Are you
LOVE, JUSTICE, WISDOM, or POWER?
Go to https://johnvoris.com/
and sign up to take a free online test
that reveals your Life Theme.

Learn to Sell What They Are Buying

Discover the Authentic Motivations of Your Prospects

John Voris

THiNK_aha_®

An Actionable Sales Journal

E-mail: info@thinkaha.com
20660 Stevens Creek Blvd., Suite 210
Cupertino, CA 95014

Published by THiNKaha®
20660 Stevens Creek Blvd., Suite 210, Cupertino, CA 95014
http://thinkaha.com
E-mail: info@thinkaha.com

This book is the authorized text for educational purposes provided by Authentic Systems LLC.

First Printing: June 2019
Hardcover ISBN: 978-1-61699-296-5 1-61699-296-4
Paperback ISBN: 978-1-61699-295-8 1-61699-295-6
eBook ISBN: 978-1-61699-294-1 1-61699-294-8
Place of Publication: Silicon Valley, California, USA
Paperback Library of Congress Number: 2018962287

Trademarks

All terms mentioned in this book that are known to be trademarks or service marks have been appropriately capitalized. Neither THiNKaha, nor any of its imprints, can attest to the accuracy of this information. Use of a term in this book should not be regarded as affecting the validity of any trademark or service mark.

Warning and Disclaimer

Every effort has been made to make this book as complete and as accurate as possible. The information provided is on an "as is" basis. The author(s), publisher, and their agents assume no responsibility for errors or omissions. Nor do they assume liability or responsibility to any person or entity with respect to any loss or damages arising from the use of information contained herein.

Acknowledgement

I would like to thank my daughters, Amanda and Jessica, for their developmental and artistic contributions; Bill Lopachuk, for his inspiration; Rachelle Onishi, for helping me structure my workshops; Tom Burns, who did my first formal reading and assisted with developing my seminar; Dr. Russ Volkman, who helped me transition into a more consumer-friendly language; Linda Hardenstein, for sharing her expertise as a Career Consultant; Melissa Wells, who assisted in preparing this book and my website; Jean Ferguson, my interoffice organizer; Mitchell Levy and his wonderful team; and of course, Jonathan Rogers, for his technical support and being a sounding board over the years.

Dedication

To my wife, Kathleen.

For her support and patience far beyond reason.

How to Read a THiNKaha® Book

A Note from the Publisher

The AHAthat/THiNKaha series is the CliffsNotes of the 21st century. These books are contextual in nature. Although the actual words won't change, their meaning will every time you read one as your context will change. Be ready, you will experience your own AHA moments as you read the AHA messages™ in this book. They are designed to be stand-alone actionable messages that will help you think about a project you're working on, an event, a sales deal, a personal issue, etc. differently. As you read this book, please think about the following:

1. It should only take 15–20 minutes to read this book the first time out. When you're reading, write in the underlined area one to three action items that resonate with you.
2. Mark your calendar to re-read this book again in 30 days.
3. Repeat step #1 and mark one to three more AHA messages that resonate. They will most likely be different than the first time. BTW: this is also a great time to reflect on the AHA messages that resonated with you during your last reading.

After reading a THiNKaha book, marking your AHA messages, re-reading it, and marking more AHA messages, you'll begin to see how these books contextually apply to you. AHAthat/ THiNKaha books advocate for continuous, lifelong learning. They will help you transform your AHAs into actionable items with tangible results until you no longer have to say AHA to these moments—they'll become part of your daily practice as you continue to grow and learn.

Mitchell Levy, The AHA Guy at AHAthat
publisher@thinkaha.com

THiNKaha®

Contents

Prologue

LOVE   JUSTICE   WISDOM   POWER

Why Is This Unique?

In 1980, I decided to rebel against all of what I had learned from traditional sales training and start over. I had used all the latest methods and techniques and still failed. From this fresh beginning, I was able to discover sales principles and methods that produced unheard-of results in this country. My new source was the European discoveries in linguistics and psychology I learned from my college studies. I turned years of failure into success.

Europeans have the answers we in America are looking for but are denied by the pressures from organizations such as the American Psychiatric Association. Several European scholars of linguistics have unraveled many mysteries surrounding human communication that still exist in this country. Communication is the number-one tool in sales, and European academics know the meaning of communication is not just found in the words we use and body language. Rather, meaning is found in the dynamics of the interpretation of symbols (Objects).

Sales Training

As a sales rep, I look at the objects surrounding my prospects and other physical evidence that will reveal their beliefs, values, and motivations. They will reveal their current worldview and what they are willing to buy and not buy. What people sell is not something a buyer sees as just another object to have and satisfy a momentary need—the sales rep has convinced a buyer that this object qualifies to become part of their identity and worthy of purchase. By assessing these real physical objects, this method is objective and not of personal opinions.

This approach is why I have been able to teach sales for over fifteen years, producing 100-percent Authentic Satisfaction. This satisfaction includes many who discovered in workshop training that they had been coerced into accepting a sales position that, now they know through this training, did not conform to their Authenticity. Now they know to get out.

As you can see, Authentic Systems is not personality dependent nor does it follow the principles taught by the sales training industry. Rather, by assembling the meaning of the objects and environment surrounding the prospect, they became the catalyst to produce Authentic Systems. In other words, by approaching what surrounds the prospect as a collection of artifacts representing his or her past decisions, I teach people how to become an Authentic Sales Archeologist.

Authentic Systems

Authentic Systems share many of the characteristics found in the sciences of archeology and forensics. These sciences have developed effective methods of analyzing objects to learn about the people who possessed them. Archeology analyzes artifacts of the past, and forensics assesses physical evidence in the present. They are able to connect objects to societies and individual people by using processes found in archeology.

From this beginning, I noticed other, larger patterns emerge. Through research, I discovered that many scholars throughout history reported similar consistencies and grouped these into categories. Indigenous people from around the world used variations of four universal human characteristics—for example, healer, teacher, visionary, and warrior. These basic categories have been used in existential psychology originating from European schools and motivational systems from Germany.

I now have a system for reading objects that collectively could be captured under what is now known as "Four Universal Virtues" that we all share.

Introduction

Is the book you are currently holding in your hands your ticket to happiness? This book contains nothing less than the system for understanding human nature and finding contentment and fulfillment in life. The key to understanding your true identity and creating a life that fulfills your purpose lies within these pages.

Unknown to you and most of your peers in sales, a battle has been raging between the European view of motivation and the American view for years. The Europeans have the answers that the American sales training industry is still looking for. Using this knowledge will catapult you from a novice salesperson to a professional. For the professional salesperson, adopting this model means you will no longer rely on intuition alone to close your sales. Instead of intuition controlling you, you will control it.

When all people have exhausted the self-help industry and want more depth, not just but including salespeople, they come to me. The self-help industry, including personality profiling, can take you only so far, which is why this book may truly be what you have been searching for. Authentic Systems is a system developed through my observations of people and the objects with which they surround themselves.

It became apparent that people gather objects that enable them to better express their inner identity. That is, when we consistently recognize that certain people identify with certain items, we find the real identity of those people.

European scholars have known for decades that objects reveal who we are. Through reading their research and my application, I have taken it from theory to practical use. By "reading" the meaning of those objects, we should find the real identity of these people. Since we surround ourselves with items that have meaning to us, I began to realize that by studying the contents of someone's home or office, one can learn something about the owner's unique perspective and life motivation.

This is exactly what I did for over thirty-five years, using my sales route as a testing ground. I first used and validated this system for twenty years while in the sales industry. Then I left sales and spent the following fifteen years helping hundreds of people find their way back to who they really are. In so doing, each of my clients has found their own unique path to happiness.

Authentic Systems is based on observation. This makes the methods and results teachable, repeatable, universal, and verifiable. In fact, I taught Authentic Systems to my daughter when she was fourteen years old. It is not dependent on theory or personality, but rather just pure observational data. For that reason, it is both logically and intuitively easy to understand. I have taught hundreds how to "read" the true motivations of themselves and others. This book is designed to introduce you to this system.

It is my hope that through the wisdom and insight contained within these pages, you will begin a truly remarkable journey in sales.

John Voris
May 2019

Learn to know the prospects you're interacting with in a way that they can relate to and trust you. This is done by using terms that resonate with their #AuthenticIdentity. #KnowYourProspects

John Voris
http://aha.pub/Learn2Sell

Share the AHA messages from this book socially by going to
http://aha.pub/Learn2Sell

Section I

Do You Really Know Your Prospect Enough to Sell Them Something?

As an American salesperson, you've never been exposed to the European approach to motivation, have you? This has never been applied to sales in the United States, until now.

Most people don't know there has been a battle between the European view of motivation and the American view. Europeans have answers the American sales training industry is still looking for. Using this knowledge will catapult you from a novice salesperson to a professional. For the professional salesperson, adopting this model means you will no longer rely on intuition alone to close your sales. Instead of intuition controlling you, you will control it.

Watch this video: http://aha.pub/Learn2SellS1

1

The European approach to motivation
is radically different from the American
approach. Know and understand this
and completely change your strategy.
#KnowYourProspects

_____

_____

_____

2

There are four virtues that all of us have: Love,
Justice, Wisdom, and Power. For each of us,
one of those four virtues is our dominant
controlling #LifeTheme. #KnowYourProspects

_____

_____

_____

3

A Love person is all about compassion,
empathy, and feelings. #KnowYourProspects

_____

_____

_____

4

A Justice person is seeking balance,
design, fairness, and harmony.
#KnowYourProspects

_____

_____

_____

5

A Wisdom person will look at an object and see if it will enhance their knowledge. #KnowYourProspects

_____

_____

_____

6

A Power person is someone who wants
to produce achievements and reach
goals over all other considerations.
#KnowYourProspects

_____

_____

_____

7

The essential element to Love is Caring,
to Justice is Symmetry, to Wisdom
is Learning, and to Power is Change.
#KnowYourProspects

_____

_____

_____

8

Our individual life themes (Love, Justice, Wisdom, or Power) look at the same object from one of these perspectives. This is what motivates someone to purchase. #KnowYourProspects

_____

_____

_____

9

Everything that surrounds your prospects are things they need in order to express their #AuthenticIdentity. Be aware of your prospect's surroundings. #KnowYourProspects

_____

_____

_____

10

Learn to know the prospects you're interacting with in a way they can relate to and trust you. This is done by using terms that resonate with their #AuthenticIdentity. #KnowYourProspects

_____

_____

_____

11

Want to increase the chance of a sale? Verbalize the benefits you are selling from the prospect's authentic perspective. #KnowYourProspects

_____

_____

_____

12

The human mind has only one need, and that is the perpetual need to express its #AuthenticIdentity. Let your prospects express theirs. #KnowYourProspects

_____

_____

_____

13

Once your prospect completely, and without any further contingencies, connects their #Authentic Identity to the object you're selling, they will definitely buy it. #KnowYourProspects

_____

_____

_____

14

Identify your prospect's authentic self. In order to appeal to them, craft your message to include their type of Authentic benefits that they'll receive when they make the purchase. #KnowYourProspects

_____

_____

_____

15

Suspend your #Authentic self long enough to see your prospect accurately. Otherwise, too many prospects will appear to be guided by your #LifeTheme. #KnowYourProspects

_____

_____

_____

16

A good salesperson is someone who understands who their prospect is and communicates with them authentically. #KnowYourProspects

---

17

When you speak in your prospect's terms, you speak to their authentic self, where you will connect to them authentically. #KnowYourProspects

_____

_____

_____

18

When salespeople connect effectively to their prospect's theme (Love, Justice, Wisdom, or Power), they increase their desire to buy to 100%. That does not mean you will sell to them, but the desire is there. #KnowYourProspects

_____

_____

_____

Humans have to express their #AuthenticIdentity, and they do it through conforming symbols of meanings, which are their basis of buying objects. #KnowYourProspects

John Voris
http://aha.pub/Learn2Sell

Share the AHA messages from this book socially by going to
http://aha.pub/Learn2Sell

Section II

Rethink Everything You Think You Know about Sales

You've read all of the sales books. And you've taken all of the courses. Have you noticed that they say the same thing over and over?

This approach is different because it is a new paradigm. And this sales approach is not being taught anywhere else in the world. European psychologists know that a sale is made when the prospect, the sales rep, and the object being sold are in alignment.

Learning this means rethinking everything you think you know about sales. If you are willing to change your understanding of your prospect, you will be able to learn their buying motivation and increase sales.

Watch this video: http://aha.pub/Learn2SellS2

19

As good salespeople, knowing how to discover our prospect's motivation will tell us what we are REALLY selling to that person. #KnowYourProspects

_____

_____

_____

20

Every object has two basic meanings to the owner: social and personal. By reading the object, you're able to read their deeper motivations. #KnowYourProspects

_____

_____

_____

21

Objects are symbols that represent abstract ideas. These symbols are what salespeople need to look for in order to know what motivates their prospect. #KnowYourProspects

22

An object's social meaning that conforms to a prospect's #AuthenticIdentity has a positive impact on them. #KnowYourProspects

23

The objects we bring into our lives are stage props through which we act out our daily dramas. #KnowYourProspects

_____

_____

_____

24

Everyone has general beliefs through which they view the world. Anything outside those beliefs is alien to them and they won't trust what does not conform to those beliefs. Do you know your prospect's worldview? #KnowYourProspects

_____

_____

_____

25

Humans have to express their
#AuthenticIdentity, and they do it through
conforming symbols of meanings,
which are their basis of buying objects.
#KnowYourProspects

_____

_____

_____

26

To increase sales, alter your sales language to the #LifeTheme you're talking to. Speak in terms of compassion, fairness, knowledge, or status. #KnowYourProspects

_____

_____

_____

27

When your prospects see themselves in the description you're giving to the object you're selling, they will want to buy. Now, convince them that they can. #KnowYourProspects

_____

_____

_____

28

Don't focus on just one aspect of your prospect; focus on the words they use, the empathy they project, their reasoning, and what they value. #KnowYourProspects

_____

_____

_____

29

Make your prospect see the object you're selling as part of who they are, so they know they must have it. #KnowYourProspects

_____

_____

_____

30

If you do door-to-door (D2D) sales, you need to notice the environment your prospect lives in to understand who your prospect is before you knock on their door. #KnowYourProspects

_____

_____

_____

When selling a product, just describe the image you believe your prospect is looking for — that is, how your prospect relates to the world.
#KnowYourProspects

John Voris
http://aha.pub/Learn2Sell

Share the AHA messages from this book socially by going to
http://aha.pub/Learn2Sell

Section III

Why Buying a Ferrari Isn't Just Buying a Ferrari

Buying an object means different things to different people. Buying a Ferrari may mean to one person, "I've got a lot of money," but to another person, buying a Ferrari means, "I'm not poor anymore."

When you are selling a Ferrari or another object, you are trying to sell a worldview. Know that your prospect is looking at your product through the filter of their worldview, waiting to hear similar language. When you as a salesperson understand this, you will change the way you relate to your prospect.

Watch this video: http://aha.pub/Learn2SellS3

31

Relatability: when you and what you are selling conforms to your prospect's #LifeTheme of Love, Justice, Wisdom, or Power. #KnowYourProspects

_____

_____

_____

32

Hear what your prospect is saying, and ask yourself, "What type of #LifeTheme would say that?" Then mirror the life theme of your prospect in your language. #KnowYourProspects

_____

_____

_____

33

Prospects spend money on objects that help them express their #AuthenticIdentity. A successful salesperson helps the prospect express their authentic self. #KnowYourProspects

_____

_____

_____

34

Speaking to the #LifeTheme of your prospect is essential for successful sales. #KnowYourProspects

_____

_____

_____

35

You're not actually selling the corporate features and functions of the object, but rather the #Relatability of you and your object to your prospect. #KnowYourProspects

_____

_____

_____

36

Manufacturers usually speak to only one of the four life themes of people (Love, Justice, Wisdom, or Power). As salespeople, you need to know how to speak to all four. #KnowYourProspects

_____

_____

_____

37

Don't always say the same thing to every prospect. A good salesperson knows how to communicate to their prospect's authentic self. Have all four scripts of Love, Justice, Wisdom, and Power available. #KnowYourProspects

_____

_____

_____

38

Prospects are not in the habit of buying things they don't know. So, sell the #Idea of your product in a way they can relate to. #KnowYourProspects

_____

_____

_____

39

Features and benefits mean nothing to the buyer if not described in terms of their #LifeTheme. Focus on the product's idea — that's what you need to sell. #KnowYourProspects

_____

_____

_____

40

Sell #Ideas that are relatable to your prospect, not what the manufacturer says you should sell. #KnowYourProspects

_____

_____

_____

41

#Ideas are the images that come to a person's mind when they look at an object. We cannot "know" any object, only the meaning communicated to us. #IdeasForSale #KnowYourProspects

_____

_____

_____

42

Objects communicate with us and
we project meaning upon them. Our
reality consists of how we relate to both.
#IdeasForSale #KnowYourProspects

_____

_____

_____

43

When selling a product, just describe the
image you believe your prospect is looking
for — that is, how your prospect relates to
the world. #KnowYourProspects

_____

_____

_____

44

As a sales manager, get your salespeople away from focusing on the four potential physical meanings of the object itself and into the abstract #Idea of the object instead. #KnowYourProspects

_____

_____

_____

45

As a salesperson, what are you really selling? You're selling the perceived benefit that is received by the person purchasing it. #KnowYourProspects

_____

_____

_____

46

If you are a salesperson, don't have just one script. The script will inevitably describe one theme. The possibility of the sale actually plummets if you use the wrong script. #KnowYourProspects

_____

_____

_____

47

After the initial training period, the script can be dropped and replaced with words that fall under the four themes: Love, Justice, Wisdom, or Power. #KnowYourProspects

_____

_____

_____

When you speak to a prospect, you should speak to their theme (love, justice, wisdom, or power), which is their belief structure and worldview. #KnowYourProspects

John Voris
http://aha.pub/Learn2Sell

Share the AHA messages from this book socially by going to
http://aha.pub/Learn2Sell

Section IV

Prospects Display
Four Distinct Buying Themes

Love, Justice, Wisdom, and Power: Each prospect has their own reasons for buying, and their motivation can be divided into these four distinct themes.

Each theme defines what the prospect values. What the prospect values impacts their motivation for buying. Once you know your prospect's buying motivations, you'll know the best way to approach them when offering what you're selling.

Watch this video: http://aha.pub/Learn2SellS4

48

It's not always about how many products you can offer; it's more about how much you can relate the product you're selling to your prospect. #KnowYourProspects

_____

_____

_____

49

The Love person is all about #Relationships with other people, so they will base their decisions on how it will affect themselves and others. #SellToTheTheme #KnowYourProspects

_____

_____

_____

50

The Justice person will base their decision on what's right, wrong, good, bad, and fair. #SellToTheTheme #KnowYourProspects

_____

_____

_____

51

A Wisdom person will base their
decision on what they know and how
much you know. #SellToTheTheme
#KnowYourProspects

_____

_____

_____

52

A Power person will base their decision on your controlled confidence in empowering them. #SellToTheTheme #KnowYourProspects

_____

_____

_____

53

Why is it important to focus on these four themes (Love, Justice, Wisdom, or Power)? Because they guide our life decisions in type and kind. #KnowYourProspects

_____

_____

_____

54

When you speak to a prospect, you should speak to their theme (Love, Justice, Wisdom, or Power), which is their belief structure and worldview. #KnowYourProspects

_____

_____

_____

55

#Ideas are flexible. Use the ideas of your product to speak to different people based on their theme (Love, Justice, Wisdom, or Power). #KnowYourProspects

_____

_____

_____

56

The perception of the buyer is typically different from the manufacturer's perceived value of the item being sold. #KnowYourProspects

_____

_____

_____

57

There's typically a disconnect between what the manufacturer is selling and what the buyer is buying. They may both be viewing the world from a different theme (Love, Justice, Wisdom, or Power). #KnowYourProspects

_____

_____

_____

58

When you have an individual who creates products that resonate with themselves, they're able to attract people from the same theme (Love, Justice, Wisdom, or Power). #KnowYourProspects

_____

_____

_____

59

When a celebrity creates or promotes a product based on who they are, people who relate to the celebrity's theme (Love, Justice, Wisdom, or Power) tend to buy. #KnowYourProspects

_____

_____

_____

60

A Marilyn Monroe dress was auctioned for $1.5 million. It's not that the dress was valuable, it was the fact that Marilyn Monroe wore it, showing the power of symbolic meaning. #KnowYourProspects

_____

_____

_____

61

Antiques can connect us symbolically
with the past and conform to our present
#LifeTheme. #KnowYourProspects

_____

_____

_____

62

Marketing typically speaks a different language than sales by grasping our innate human general motivations often missed by the sales training industry. It is the successful sales agent who understands the human element. #KnowYourProspects

_____

_____

_____

63

Quota systems are deadly. The agent looks beyond the prospect and focuses on the number of sales needed to keep employed. The prospect vanishes in importance. #KnowYourProspects

_____

_____

_____

64

First, describe the benefits in the language of all four themes until interest is sparked. #KnowYourProspects

_____

_____

_____

65

The Love #LifeTheme is about compassion and empathy. These are the people who care about another person's well-being, and it will be the basis of their purchase. #SellToTheTheme #KnowYourProspects

_____

_____

_____

A person may lead into a decision by thinking about it, but in the end, their decision comes from something beyond language, found in the hidden life themes of love, justice, wisdom, and power. #SellToTheTheme #KnowYourProspects

John Voris
http://aha.pub/Learn2Sell

Share the AHA messages from this book socially by going to
http://aha.pub/Learn2Sell

Section V

"That Outfit Is So You!"
The Hidden Secret

Prospects are always buying who they are. As a salesperson, it is up to you to figure out who they are. If you are a clothing salesperson, for example, and a woman comes to you dressed conservatively, you would recommend a conservative outfit to her. People buy objects that mean something to them, and that decision stems from who the person is or what their authentic identity is. And it all starts with the prospect's theme.

Watch this video: http://aha.pub/Learn2SellS5

66

Your opportunity for a sale dramatically increases when you symbolically connect the meaning of the object you're selling to the #LifeTheme of the buyer.

67

The Love #LifeTheme focuses on personal growth and self-development. It's focused on one's self and others. #SellToTheTheme #KnowYourProspects

---

68

The Justice #LifeTheme is about balance, morality, and ethics, involving both Wisdom and Love. Justice people have empathy; they empathize with people and help them find answers. #SellToTheTheme #KnowYourProspects

_____

_____

_____

69

The Justice person is focused on both Wisdom and Love. Their need to know occurs in order to correct what is causing discomfort. #SellToTheTheme #KnowYourProspects

_____

_____

_____

70

The Power #LifeTheme is about personal empowerment and the empowerment of others. They're action oriented. #SellToTheTheme #KnowYourProspects

_____

_____

_____

71

The Wisdom #LifeTheme is about knowledge and applying it to everyday life. #SellToTheTheme #KnowYourProspects

---

72

A person may lead into a decision by thinking about it, but in the end, their decision comes from something beyond language, found in the hidden life themes of Love, Justice, Wisdom, and Power. #SellToTheTheme #KnowYourProspects

---

73

What links objects to our personal meaning of them? It is our brand of symmetry revealed in our reasons for binding them together. Reasoning, therefore, is a tool to justify our decisions that direct our buying motivation. What type of reasoning does your prospect use? #KnowYourProspects

---

74

Being right is the glue that holds our #AuthenticIdentity together. What kind of "right" we are reveals our #LifeTheme and our buying motivations. #KnowYourProspects

---

75

If it helps, imagine that people in each #LifeTheme see the world through certain "glasses." Love has green glasses, representing nature. Wisdom wears yellow, representing mental activity. Justice has blue, representing tranquility. Power wears red, representing high energy. #KnowYourProspects

---

76

If you want to sell something to somebody else: 1) Recognize the language belonging to one of the themes (Love, Justice, Wisdom, or Power). 2) Describe what you're selling in those terms. 3) Use Authentic Reasoning. #KnowYourProspects

77

The objects sitting in a room are symbols that represent an #Idea. Look for these symbols to know more about your prospect. #KnowYourProspects

_____

_____

_____

78

Begin with thinking about the symbolic meaning of the overall environment of your prospect. From the neighborhood to the office building or house you find them in, they are all signs of who they are. #KnowYourProspects

_____

_____

79

Include the geographical symbolic meaning that surrounds your prospect, and search for conforming patterns displayed by others in the area. #KnowYourProspects

_____

_____

_____

80

#Symbols can be found in the city, street, house, and building. Symbols are everywhere; all you have to do is pay attention. #KnowYourProspects

_____

_____

_____

81

A #Symbol is an object that has meaning in itself. We can see the object as a physical thing, but there's meaning to it. Do you know the meaning of the objects surrounding your prospect? #KnowYourProspects

---

82

#Symbols are visible objects that represent invisible ideas. An expensive car is a symbol of wealth. Wealth itself is an "invisible" concept. #KnowYourProspects

---

83

Your prospect's mind functions by processing #Symbols, which are visible representations of invisible concepts. #UnderstandTheSymbols #KnowYourProspects

_____

_____

_____

84

We need to understand the #Symbols around us in order to relate to and be more sociable with our prospects. #KnowYourProspects

_____

_____

_____

85

In selling, your prospect is surrounded by previous decisions represented by objects of Symbolic Meaning. Do you know the symbolic meaning surrounding your prospect? #KnowYourProspects

_____

_____

_____

86

Look at the #Symbols around the environment and the way your prospect is speaking. Those are hints to get to know your prospect better. #KnowYourProspects

_____

_____

_____

87

Objects around us are #Symbols that help us find meaning, purpose, and our potential, all of which help us find happiness. #KnowYourProspects

_____

_____

_____

88

A salesperson needs to pick up on their prospect's #AuthenticIdentity and base the way they sell on what best conforms to their prospect. #KnowYourProspects

_____

_____

_____

89

The symbols that surround your prospect relate to each other by each resonating with their unique #AuthenticIdentity. #KnowYourProspects

_____

_____

_____

90

The things you buy are the things you liked at one time. How do you know you liked them? There is no logic there, but the answer to that question reveals your #LifeTheme. #KnowYourProspects

_____

_____

_____

91

#AuthenticSystems is a very powerful mental exercise and should never be revealed to the prospect, or the sales rep's sincerity would be in jeopardy. #KnowYourProspects

_____

_____

_____

92

By following simple procedures, you will always be able to isolate the prospect's #LifeTheme. #KnowYourProspects

_____

_____

_____

93

All people live with all four themes. Your job is to find which one dominates the other three. #KnowYourProspects

_____

_____

_____

94

Remember, you and the objects that surround you are symbols of meaning to your prospect as well. Don't dress too far beneath or above your average buying customer. #KnowYourProspects

_____

_____

_____

95

If you're looking at a prospect and
using their words associated with Love,
Justice, Wisdom, or Power, you become
a conforming symbol in their eyes.
#BeASymbol #KnowYourProspects

_____

_____

_____

96

When a prospect makes a decision based on their #Life Theme (Love, Justice, Wisdom, and Power), you are helping them affirm their #AuthenticIdentity. #KnowYourProspects

_____

_____

_____

97

We create and confirm our
#AuthenticIdentity when we make
decisions. Do you know yours?
#KnowYourProspects

_____

_____

_____

98

When a prospect makes a final decision to buy, they are buying through the lens of their one and only true identity (Love, Justice, Wisdom, or Power) that lies beneath their personality. #KnowYourProspects

_____

_____

_____

99

If the salesperson does not offer enough authentic description to allow the prospect's #AuthenticIdentity to surface, the prospect will not be able to make a confident purchase. #KnowYourProspects

_____

_____

_____

100

There are two aspects of human history: that which changes and that which stays the same. Love, Justice, Wisdom, and Power stay the same. What changes is how we manifest them in the physical world. #KnowYourProspects

_____

_____

101

Prospects end up looking for the same personal meaning over and over. That's why salespeople need to look at the pattern to determine the prospect's #AuthenticIdentity. #KnowYourProspects

_____

_____

_____

102

The #LifeTheme is like a picture frame, with our #AuthenticIdentity as the picture within the frame. This is who we are as a person. What's your Authentic Identity? #KnowYourProspects

_____

_____

_____

103

As a salesperson, you need to ask the right questions to allow other people to see your product or service through the eyes of their #LifeTheme. #KnowYourProspects

_____

_____

_____

104

The secret is to speak from one of your own Archetypes of Love, Justice, Wisdom, or Power to your prospect's #LifeTheme. You have all the tools to make authentic contact. #KnowYourProspects

_____

_____

_____

105

People talk in a certain way to other people, depending on who they are. You don't talk to your mother the way you talk to your significant other. So, don't talk the same way to every prospect. #KnowYourProspects

---

106

People act in a certain way in different places, depending on location. You don't act the same way at a cocktail lounge as you do in a church. Don't act the same way with every prospect. #KnowYourProspects

---

107

When the prospect makes the connection
between a certain object and its meaning,
that shows who they are as a person.
#KnowYourProspects

_____

_____

_____

108

When the prospect, salesperson, and object
being sold are aligned, you have a sale.
#KnowYourProspects

_____

_____

_____

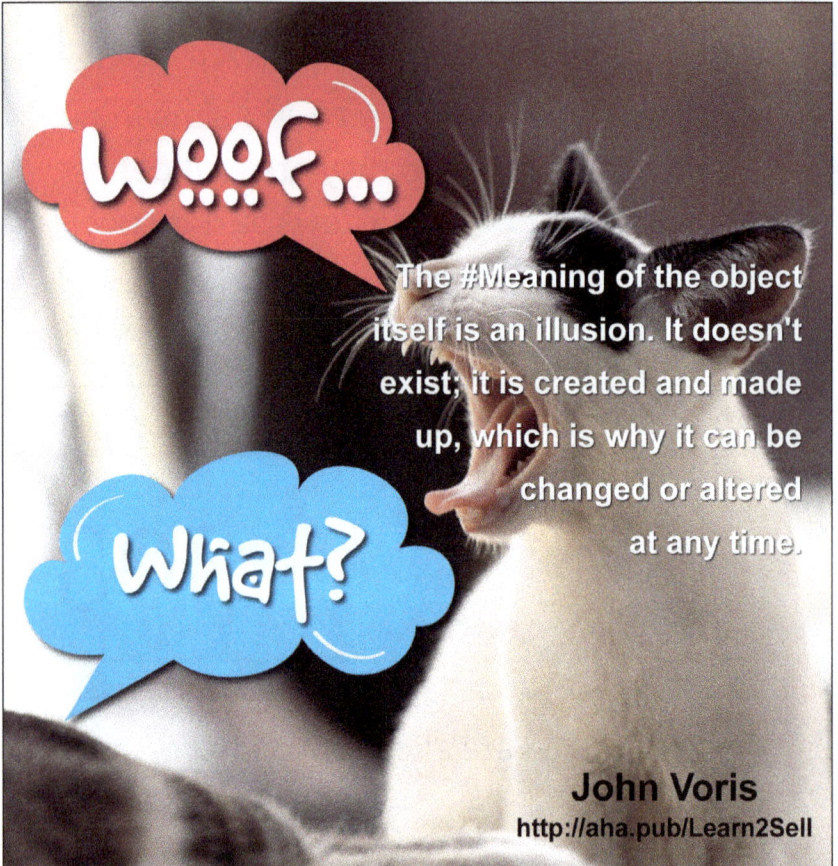

Share the AHA messages from this book socially by going to
http://aha.pub/Learn2Sell

Section VI

You Wouldn't Cast Joe Pesci for a Role Written for John Wayne

Any salesperson can easily talk to a prospect with whom they share the same life theme. An experienced and effective Authentic salesperson, however, is also aware of the other three themes and can recognize them in a prospect. These sales reps know how to speak with all four in their language. In contrast, talking with a prospect using the wrong theme-language would be like casting Joe Pesci in a role written for John Wayne. A prospect will only know, like, and trust you when you use their theme language.

Watch this video: http://aha.pub/Learn2SellS6

109

You need to sell in a way that conforms to your prospect in order for them to know, like, trust, and buy from you. http://aha.pub/TEDtalk #KnowYourProspects

_____

_____

_____

110

There's nothing to change about you, only something to be aware of. Once you are aware of your prospect's #LifeTheme, you'll know how to sell to them. #KnowYourProspects

_____

_____

_____

111

The #Meaning of the object itself is an illusion. It doesn't exist; it is created and made up, which is why it can be changed or altered at any time. #KnowYourProspects

_____

_____

_____

112

Talking as an #Authentic person is better than reading a script, because a script is written by somebody else. #BeYouDoYou #KnowYourProspects

_____

_____

_____

113

A script doesn't resonate with the prospect you're talking to — it's artificial. #BeAuthentic #KnowYourProspects

_____

_____

_____

114

A script is only good for a salesperson who is new to the industry and does not know what to say. Once the essence of the script is mastered, transform it into your language and deliver an authentic message. #KnowYourProspects

_____

_____

_____

115

In the movies, the script and the actor need to conform to the character portrayed to make it believable. The same is true for selling. #KnowYourProspects

_____

_____

_____

116

The symbolic meaning of all objects is
flexible. Practice describing the product or
service you're selling from the perspective
of all four life themes. #KnowYourProspects

_____

_____

_____

117

From a visual perspective, the person who is selling needs to paint a picture that is appealing to their prospect's #AuthenticIdentity. #KnowYourProspects

_____

_____

_____

118

From an audio perspective, the person who is selling needs a series of words and content that resonates with their prospect's life themes. #KnowYourProspects

_____

_____

_____

119

Listen to your prospect's stories. Love Theme may see taxes as money diverted away from the wellbeing of the family. Justice may see taxes as being unfair. Wisdom may see taxes spent unwisely. Power may see taxes as a reduction of personal control. #KnowYourProspects

---

120

Being authentic means being in compliance with your #LifeTheme. If you're not being your authentic self in relating to prospects, you won't be trusted. #KnowYourProspects

---

121

It's important for the salesperson to truly
relate to their prospect in the #LifeTheme
(Love, Justice, Wisdom, and Power)
that the prospect is in, and it has to be
done with integrity and authenticity.
#KnowYourProspects

_____

_____

_____

Pre-qualify your prospect first before you meet, to understand the best approach to sell to them. #SellToTheTheme #KnowYourProspects

John Voris
http://aha.pub/Learn2Sell

Share the AHA messages from this book socially by going to
http://aha.pub/Learn2Sell

Section VII

Elementary, Dear Watson!

As a detective, Sherlock Holmes trained himself to be a great observer of facts, objects, and personalities. From physical evidence, he was able to capture human behavior. Similarly, as an authentic sales rep, you observe details about your prospects and see the patterns revealing the binding agent—Their Life Theme.

Watch this video: http://aha.pub/Learn2SellS7

122

It's important for a salesperson to discover the hidden buying motivations of their prospects. Do you have a process to do that? #KnowYourProspects

_____

_____

_____

123

Prospects need to bring objects into their lives that express who they are, and that's what a sales rep has to understand and be aware of. #KnowYourProspects

_____

_____

_____

124

One #LifeTheme (Love, Justice, Wisdom, and Power) dominates our life, guiding our view of the world and shaping who we are as a person. Which theme prevails in your prospects? #KnowYourProspects

_____

_____

_____

125

To be a successful sales rep, you need to be able to mirror your buyer's #LifeTheme, what's around them, and the #Symbols they use to represent themselves. #KnowYourProspects

_____

_____

_____

126

As a salesperson, you need to learn how to offer the visible and sell the invisible in order to strengthen your chances for a sale.
#KnowYourProspects

127

Objects, people, and events are stage props that point to who your prospects are and what their life is about.
#KnowYourProspects

128

Love, Justice, Wisdom, and Power form the source of all our decisions. Do you know your prospect's #AuthenticIdentity? #KnowYourProspects

_____

_____

_____

129

The things, places, and people around us are #SymbolsOfMeaning, conforming to our one and only true identity. #KnowYourProspects

_____

_____

_____

130

Sales is about determining a prospect's #AuthenticIdentity by understanding the dominating #Meaning of the objects surrounding them. #KnowYourProspects

_____

_____

_____

131

Your prospects will identify themselves in the description of the object you're selling, which is why it's important to adapt the way you sell to your prospect's #AuthenticIdentity. #KnowYourProspects

_____

_____

_____

132

Learn how to speak to the meaning
your prospects are communicating.
There is nothing to change in yourself,
only something to be aware of.
#KnowYourProspects

_____

_____

_____

133

Pre-qualify your prospect first before you
meet, to understand the best approach
to sell to them. #SellToTheTheme
#KnowYourProspects

_____

_____

_____

134

Know that your prospect also had to personally pre-qualify their skills, abilities, and motivations before assuming their current job. Learn their job description and know your prospect. #KnowYourProspects

_____

_____

_____

135

To be social in person, you have to be relatable. Prospects trust relatable people. Are you? #KnowYourProspects

_____

_____

_____

136

To be relatable as a salesperson, you need to let your prospects express who they are and conform to that expression. #KnowYourProspects

_____

_____

_____

137

When you speak to your prospect using his or her #LifeTheme, you are in fact engaged in #AuthenticRapport. The prospect is hearing their own brand of descriptive reasoning. This promotes harmony, linguistic agreement, mutual understanding, and empathy. #KnowYourProspects

---

138

You don't need to know what your prospect is literally thinking. You do need to know how they think based on their #LifeTheme. #KnowYourProspects

---

139

Are you listening and sharing in the prospect's #AuthenticLanguage? #KnowYourProspects

_____

_____

_____

140

Prospects feel comfortable and open
to those who hear them vs. those
who don't. #ListenToYourProspects
#KnowYourProspects

_____

_____

_____

Appendix

Definitions

Alignment with Prospect
We all **Know, Like, and Trust** the values and meaning we identify as ourselves. If done correctly, the values and meaning of the prospect, the object or service sold, and the sales rep become aligned through conforming verbal descriptions.

Authentic Life Theme
A Life Theme is one of four Universal Virtues that dominate our world perspective and give form to both our moral and ethical constructions, which are the foundations of our Authentic Identity.

The Authentic Identity
The Authentic Identity is a stabilizing process of psychic elements, including Love, Justice, Wisdom, and Power, that continuously flow into a unified, individual identity. This identity is the force that drives our external personality.

Authentic Meaning
Our Authentic Identity develops by transforming our surrounding Social Meaning into a unique unified conformity designed to manifest our Personal Authentic Meaning.

Authentic Rapport
This occurs when an individual is able to acknowledge and affirm the Authentic Identity beneath the personality of another through using the qualities of their own Authentic Identity.

Being Authentic
This is to freely express meaning, purpose, and action that conforms to your Life Theme—to generate overall life contentment with momentary feelings of happiness, occasioned by bursts of joy.

Conforming Symbols of Meaning
The meaning and values attached to the object or service sold, that conforms and reflects those meaning and values possessed by the prospect.

Expression of Need
The Law of Authentic Expression: the human mind has only one need, the need to stabilize, enhance, and express our Authentic Identity through conforming symbols of meaning.

Regardless of who you are—what culture, race, ethnic group, time in history, or country you belong to—no one can avoid expressing their identity. We express ourselves through the objects we possess, by the people we associate with, and by participating in events.

An Authentic Sales Representative
An Authentic sales representative is an object in the eyes of the prospect who should reflect the meaning and values that best conform to that prospect.

Social Meaning
We are born into a preexisting environment that has been defined by society.

Symbols of Meaning
Every thing that has a name is a symbol representing meaning greater than itself. Human expression is manifested through our relationship with the meaning and values we hold for objects, events, and ideas. A sales rep is always selling the meaning and values that best resonate with the prospect, which are attached to objects, events, and ideas.

About the Author

John Voris was a cold-call salesperson for over twenty years. He used what he learned from his philosophy degree at the University of California at Berkeley to create a system of selling that still works with greater consistency than what the sales training industry has to offer. This system reveals who is really going to buy and how best to sell to them based on the objects and symbols they surround themselves with.

John Voris has an extensive library that you can see in this video: http://aha.pub/JohnVorisLibrary

AHAthat ®

THiNKaha has created AHAthat for you to share content from this book.

- ➲ Share each AHA message socially: http://aha.pub/Learn2Sell
- ➲ Share additional content: https://AHAthat.com
- ➲ Info on authoring: https://AHAthat.com/Author

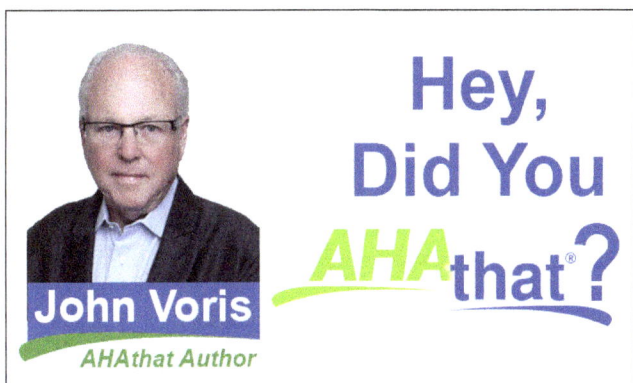

Hey, Did You AHAthat ®?

John Voris
AHAthat Author

www.ingramcontent.com/pod-product-compliance
Lightning Source LLC
Chambersburg PA
CBHW062041200326
41519CB00017B/5099